# CRAFTS
## for
## Revamping
## Your room

written by

Susannah Blake

WAYLAND

First published in 2012 by Wayland
Copyright © Wayland 2012

Wayland
338 Euston Road
London NW1 3BH

Wayland Australia
Hachette Children's Books
Level 17/207
Kent Street
Sydney, NSW 2000

Editors: Julia Adams; Katie Woolley
Craft stylist: Annalees Lim
Designer: Rocket Design
Photographer: Simon Pask, N1 Studios

The website addresses (URLs) included in this book were valid at the time of going to press. However, it is possible that contents or addresses may have changed since the publication of this book No responsibility for any such changes can be accepted by either the author or the Publisher.

British Library Cataloguing in Publication Data
Blake, Susannah.
   Crafts for revamping your room. -- (Eco chic)
   1. Interior decoration--Juvenile literature. 2. Bedrooms--
   Juvenile literature. 3. Handicraft--Juvenile literature.
   I. Title II. Series
   747.7'7-dc23

ISBN 978 0 7502 6844 8

Printed in China

Wayland is a division of Hachette Children's Books,
an Hachette UK company.

www.hachette.co.uk

Picture acknowledgements:
All step-by-step craft photography: Simon Pask, N1 Studios;
images used throughout for creative graphics: Shutterstock.

Dear diary
Page 8

Bedroom cabinet
Page 16

# Contents

Learn stitches
Page 30

Beanbag
bookends
Page 6

# Bedroom makeover

All these fab crafts are made from stuff that usually gets chucked out!

The world of interior design is a fickle thing, with yesterday's must-have becoming today's throw-away. But it needn't be that way! This book shows you the art of upcycling by using clever tricks to transform something old into something stylish and new.

## Dapper decorations and fashionable furnishings

From bunting, door signs and wall art to cushions, book ends and doorstops, there's no end to the bedroom accessories that you can make from recycled materials. Reuse fabrics from old clothes, bedding and curtains. Reclaim beads and baubles from broken or discarded jewellery, snip buttons and sequins off old clothes, save ribbons from gifts and packaging, and leftover wool from knitting projects or an unravelled jumper or scarf. Set aside decorative paper such as used wrapping paper, magazines, newspapers and stationery that you could recycle and use to decorate projects.

As well as being great for your room, the crafts in this book make super presents!

# Funky furniture

Furniture that is perfect for reclaiming, renovating and revamping is all too often thrown on the landfill heap and rejected in favour of something brand new. So stop that trend and make it work for you! Furniture can be repainted or refreshed and decorated with scrap paper (see page 17). An old armchair or sofa can be covered with a pretty throw. And simply redressing an old bed with a bright quilt and funky cushions can transform a bedroom.

You may have furniture already that you can bring back to life with some clever crafting, but if you don't, there are lots of places to search out pre-loved pieces. Start off by looking in car boot sales, charity shops and second-hand furniture stores. The internet can also be a great source with websites where you can look for local goods that are no longer wanted and websites where you can pick up furniture very cheaply in an online auction. In all cases, make sure you have an adult's permission and help in sourcing furniture.

Don't be trashy – recycle!

# Beanbag bookends

## You will need

★ scissors
★ ruler
★ sturdy fabric, such as denim or corduroy
★ needle and thread
★ scrap fabric
★ ribbon
★ buttons
★ dried beans, lentils or grains, for filling
★ funnel

**K**eep your books in order with these funky beanbag bookends! You can make the beanbags using fabric from old clothes, and decorate them with reclaimed ribbons and buttons. You can use a bag of rice, lentils or dried beans that's out of date and no good for cooking. They're ideal for filling the beanbags.

**1**

Cut out 12 10 cm x 10 cm squares from the sturdy fabric.

**2**

Cut out shapes, such as hearts or butterflies, from the denim or any other fabric you may have. Sew the shapes on to at least two of the squares, along with ribbons and buttons to decorate.

**3**

Choose six squares for each bookend. Lay four of the squares in a row and place a square on each side of the strip to make a cross shape. Then flip each square so that the back of the fabric is showing.

**4**

Use a running stitch (see page 30) to sew the edges of the squares together. Leave an inch open on the final seam.

**5**

Turn the cube inside out so that all the seams are on the inside. Then use a funnel to fill with beans, lentils or grains.

**6**

Sew up the final seam, tucking the edges in.

The more squares you decorate, the more different looks you can create. Simply rotate the bookends each day to find the design that suits your mood!

# Dear diary...

Create your very own personal journal that fastens shut with a clever button and ribbon tie to keep your secrets safe. Collect unused scrap paper that's suitable for writing on for the inside pages, such as envelopes, coloured wrapping paper and old packaging. Scraps of fabric or felt from old clothes are ideal for decorating the cover.

## You will need

- ★ scissors
- ★ card from a cereal packet
- ★ sturdy fabric or denim
- ★ scraps of fabric or felt, ribbons and buttons to decorate
- ★ needle and thread
- ★ fabric glue
- ★ plain scrap paper
- ★ hole punch
- ★ button(s) and ribbon to fasten the diary with

**1** Cut the card into two 22 cm x 31 cm rectangles. Then cut out two 25 cm x 34 cm pieces of sturdy fabric. Sew scraps of fabric, ribbons and buttons onto one of them to decorate. Sew a large button (or two on top of each other) on the right hand side of the decorated cover.

**2** Use fabric glue to stick each piece of fabric to a card rectangle, folding the fabric over to make a neat edge. Leave to dry completely. Then stick a smaller rectangle of card on to cover the glued edges.

## Paper recycling

Even though paper is easily recycled, much of it ends up in landfill. What many people don't realise is that paper can take between five and 15 years to break down.

As the paper decomposes in landfills it can create methane gas, which is highly combustible and dangerous.

**3**

Cut the scrap paper into 15 cm x 21 cm rectangles, then stack them neatly. Working with a few pieces of paper at a time, punch six holes along one edge. Make sure that the holes are in the same position on all the pieces of paper.

**4**

Insert the pages between the front and back cover, ensuring the holes match up. Sew through the cardboard and the holes in the paper to bind the book together.

**5**

Tie a ribbon around the book and fasten it into place by looping it around the button.

Use a thread colour that contrasts nicely with the colour of the cover.

You can reuse this diary over and over again — just cut the thread, repace the pages and sew everything back together.

9

# Personalised door sign

Let everyone know who sleeps here with this funky personalised door sign! You only need a DVD case, photos and scrap paper. Be super chic by choosing colours that match your bedroom décor.

## You will need

★ DVD case
★ scissors
★ scrap paper, such as wrapping paper, coloured card or magazines
★ photos
★ 40cm string or ribbon

**1**

Remove the original paper sleeve from the DVD case. Use it as a template to cut out a piece of scrap paper that is slightly smaller, and one that is the same size.

**2**

Decorate the smaller piece of paper with shapes cut out of scrap paper. Alternatively, you might want to make a collage with photos of family and friends, or a big picture of yourself with some pretty shapes. When you are finished decorating, stick this piece of paper onto the one that is the same size as the DVD sleeve.

## Recycling photographs

Photographic paper can't be recycled like other paper products. The chemicals used in the paper and thin layer of polythene that coats the photo clog up the recycling process at paper mills.

Although this is bad news in one way, it gives you loads of opportunities to be really creative in making the most of your photos in projects such as this one.

**3**

Slide this new sleeve into the DVD case, then lay the string or ribbon along the spine. Snap the case shut and tie the ends of the string or ribbon together to make a hanging loop.

It's amazing what you can find lying around. We even used an old map for these heart shapes!

If you decide to cut up some of your old photos, make sure you ask a grown up first – they might like to keep them!

**4** Hang the sign on your bedroom door!

# Pretty as a picture

## Finding a picture frame

If you don't have a picture frame at home, look out for one in charity shops and car boot sales. They're a great place to hunt out pre-loved items for you to recycle and revamp and usually cost very little.

Become an artist and create your very own artwork for your bedroom. Take an old picture frame and create a brand new picture to go inside it using scrap paper, such as graph paper, old envelopes, magazines and newspapers.

## You will need

★ sandpaper (optional)
★ acrylic paint
★ paintbrush
★ scrap paper, buttons
★ glue
★ scissors
★ card from a cereal packet

**1**

Carefully remove the back and glass from the picture frame. You may want to sand the frame to make the paint stick to it well. Then paint with acrylic paint and leave to dry.

**2**

Cut out a piece of paper to fit inside the frame. Create a collage picture by glueing shapes on top, leaving plenty of space around the outside for a mount.

**3**

To make a mount, cut out a piece of card the same size as the picture. Mark a rectangle inside leaving a border of at least 2 cm. Cut out the centre to create the mount.

**4**

Paint the mount in a colour that goes well with those used in the picture. Set it aside to dry.

**5**

Place the mount on the picture, then slip into the frame and clip back together. Hang it on your bedroom wall!

# Buttoned wool cushion

This project is a fantastic way to give a new lease of life to an old cardigan. The buttoned front gives a stylish finish with almost no effort at all! Use an old cushion or cushion pad for the filling.

## You will need

★ an old buttoned cardigan
★ cushion pad
★ dress-making pins
★ scissors
★ needle and thread

**1**
Turn the cardigan inside out and lay it flat on a table. Place the cushion pad on the cardigan and mark its shape using dress-making pins.

**2**
Cut around the pins to make the basic cushion shape. Make sure you leave a border around the pins of about 2 cm.

Never throw your worn-out jumpers away. Even if they have holes you can still recycle the wool.

**3**

Using a running stitch (see page 30), sew all the way around the edge of the pins. Repeat to give a double layer of extra-strong stitches.

**4**

Unbutton the front of the cardigan and turn it the right way round, so that the seams are inside. Insert the cushion and button up to create the finished cushion!

You can even replace the buttons to give the cushions a more stylish look.

## Disposable fashion

The fads of fashion contribute a million tonnes of waste to landfill every year, so it's a great idea to recycle old clothes in any way you can.

Many old clothes are perfect for transforming into soft furnishings.

Use your imagination and see what else you can find to turn yesterday's style statement into today's chic interior!

These cardigans had pockets. On a cushion, they are great for storing knick-knacks.

# Bedroom cabinet

Upcycle your tired old bedroom cabinet and turn it into the centrepiece of your room! All you need is a little paint and some scrap paper. Search out coloured scrap paper such as magazines, newspapers, junk mail, leaflets and flyers that will complement the other colours in your bedroom. Before you start, check that you are allowed to renovate the cabinet!

**2**

Cut the scrap paper into shapes. You might want to use them to create a little scene or a colourful collage.

**1**

If necessary, lightly sand the bedside cabinet to help the paint stick to the surface. Then paint with acrylic paint and leave to dry.

The paint will cover better if you use a lighter shade of paint as an undercoat. Perhaps you have some that needs using up?

**3**

When the cabinet is completely dry, stick the shapes on in your chosen design using PVA glue.

### Furniture dump

Research by the Furniture Reuse Network has shown that local councils in the UK send around 10 million reusable items of furniture to landfill in a single year.

**4**

Paint a thin layer of PVA glue over the whole cabinet to seal your design and leave to dry completely.

We painted this cabinet using tester pots. You can get these for free or very little money in DIY shops.

**17**

# Bunting!

Nothing cheers up a bedroom like a string of bunting! Whether it's in bright colours or seaside stripes, bunting is a great way to add a touch of fun to your room. Pick out some old clothes that don't fit you anymore so that you can turn happy memories into funky interior fashion.

**1**

25 CM

Cut the jeans into triangles (about 25 cm high and 20 cm wide). You will need at least five triangles, and it is ideal to end up with an odd, rather than an even number.

**2**

Cut out shapes or letters from the scrap material. You can make their edges look pretty by adding a blanket stitch (see page 31).

Hang the bunting up around your bedroom!

**3**

Sew the shapes onto the triangles. If you have beads, you can attach them to the bottom of each triangle.

**4**

Sew the top of each triangle to the ribbon with about 3 cm between each one. If you only have short bits of ribbon, sew them together to make one long piece before attaching the triangles.

## Broken beads

If you break a necklace or bracelet, don't despair. Pick up the beads and store them in a jar. They'll be great for adding decoration to bunting or similar furnishings, such as cushions or mobiles.

You can personalise your bunting by spelling your name across it!

# Box of treasures

Whether you need a jewellery box to keep your beads and bangles in, or just a special place to store your favourite things, this beautiful box is a must for every bedroom.

## You will need

★ shoe box
★ PVA glue
★ scissors
★ colourful scrap paper, such as wrapping paper, leftover wallpaper or magazines
★ small cardboard boxes from food packaging
★ ribbon

**2**

Place the small cardboard boxes inside the shoe box to create compartments within the box. If necessary, cut down the height of the boxes so that they fit inside the shoe box.

**1**

Coat the lid of the shoe box in a thin layer of PVA glue and cover with strips of scrap paper. Leave to dry completely.

If you dont have any coloured or patterned paper, you can try cutting up magazines.

## Repackage your packaging

Food and consumer goods create a vast amount of waste due to packaging. Often goods are contained within several layers of packaging. This may be to protect the product on its long journey to the consumer, but these numerous layers of packaging also find their way to the growing heaps of landfill. How many different ways can you think of to reclaim and reuse this excess packaging?

**3**

Use the scrap paper to decorate the boxes. Then stick them inside the shoe box.

**4**

Use the ribbon to wrap around the box and fasten it shut.

To make these cute butterflies, just layer butterfly shapes in different sizes and colours and stick their centre to the box.

You can use your box to collect fabric, buttons and ribbons that you might like to use for other projects.

21

# Cute CD hanger

Damaged or used CDs are a tricky thing to recycle, but with their shiny, reflective appearance there are loads of ways you can use them to glam up everyday objects. This cute hanger will add a bit of sparkle to any boudoir!

## You will need

★ 5-7 old CDs
★ scrap paper or magazines
★ pencil
★ scissors
★ glue
★ ribbon
★ sticky tape
★ beads

**1** Using a CD as a template, draw circles on the backs of scrap paper or magazine images and cut them out.

**2** Cut out pretty flower shapes and stick them onto the circles.

22

**3**

Stick the decorated circles onto the CDs.

**4**

Add beads to one end of the ribbon and tie a knot. If you only have short pieces of ribbon, use a needle and thread to sew them together to make a piece long enough for your CDs.

**5**

Make a loop at the other end of the ribbon, then stick the ribbon to the backs of the CDs with sticky tape. Now it's ready to hang up!

Why not have pictures of your best freinds in the centre of your CD flowers?

# Window mobile

Take nature as your inspiration to make this beautiful leafy mobile. Watch the leaves spin in the breeze, and reflect the sunshine on their shiny surface. At night they will shine in the glow of the lightbulb in your bedroom lamp.

## You will need

- ★ wool or embroidery thread
- ★ CD
- ★ images taken from old magazines or scrap paper
- ★ sticky tape
- ★ scissors
- ★ hole punch

**1**

Wind wool or embroidery thread around the CD to cover the shiny surface.

**2**

Cut the scrap paper into leaf shapes. You can make them all kinds of different shapes and sizes.

## Making the most of old CDs

Pass CDs on to someone else who might enjoy them, or give them to a charity shop. Sell them at a car boot sale or put an ad in your local corner shop. Alternatively, these shining discs make great bird scarers when hung over your veggie patch or in fruit trees. Whatever you do, don't just throw them away – look for a new home or use for them.

People throw away lots of old CDs. If you haven't got any yourself, ask around!

**3**

Carefully cover both sides of each leaf with sticky tape. Snip away any excess tape.

If you use tissue paper for your leaves, the light will shine through them like stained glass.

**4**

Using the hole punch, stamp a hole in the top of each leaf. Then attach each of them to a piece of wool or embroidery thread.

**5**

Attach the leaves to the CD using a slightly longer piece of wool or thread for each one. Fix four equal lengths of wool to the top of the CD and knot the ends together to hang up your mobile.

# Owl door stop

**You will need**

★ pillowcase
★ scissors
★ lentils, rice or dried beans, for filling
★ wadding

★ needle and thread
★ scrap fabric from old clothes
★ 2–4 buttons

Make this cute owl door stop to keep your door open... or closed! Use an old pillow case or fabric from a shirt, dress or skirt. If you like dress-making or sewing, you may have some suitable scraps left over from a previous project. An old cushion or puffy jacket are ideal sources of wadding.

**2**

Cut out shapes from scrap fabric to make the background for the face, the eyes, the beak and the feathers. Sew the shapes onto the front of the pillowcase and add two (or four) buttons for the eyes.

**1**

Cut the pillowcase in half and reserve the closed end. You can use the open end for another project.

**3**

Fill the bottom of the pillowcase with a layer of lentils, rice or dried beans, then fill the rest with wadding. Sew across the top to enclose the filling materials.

**4**

Tie the two top corners using some thread to create ears.

## Make the most of your storecupboard

If you don't keep track of your storecupboard staples such as couscous, lentils or rice, you can easily find that a packet has gone past its sell-by date. Rather than throwing it away, why not use the old grains or pulses for craft projects like this one.

**5**

Depending on the design of the cushion cover you have, you could make a dog, a cat or any other animal to guard your door!

You can also make mini owls out of the leftover cushion cover to use as paper weights.

# Style your bedroom!

Transforming your room by using new accessories and colour is one of the best ways of expressing yourself. And the good news is, it doesn't need to be wasteful or contribute to the ever-growing mountains of landfill. By recycling, reclaiming and reusing you can make everything out of nothing and give a new lease of life to items that might otherwise have ended up on the rubbish tip.

## Embrace your own interior style

Once you've decided what you need, think about colour and the kind of accessories and furniture you like. Have the confidence in your own likes and dislikes and create a look that's true to your own taste and style. Think about colours you like and reclaim, recycle and reuse materials in those shades to create a coordinated look. Or if you prefer a hodge-podge of colour and pattern, embrace your quirky side and go for it!

## Make it all about you

Before you start on any makeover, think about what you like and what you're like! Are you a girly girl who likes everything pretty and pink, are you a tom boy who loves sport and the outdoors, are you nature-mad, or do you love reading and studying hard at school?

Once you've decided on these basics, think about what kind of bedroom accessories you need. Do you need a desk for doing homework? Do you need a dressing table for trying out new hairstyles? Do you need bookends to keep your books in order and a diary to write down all your personal thoughts? Do you need cushions and beanbags to hang out on with your friends?

This box of treasures looks fab, but there are so many other ways you could decorate it — paint, foils, or even glitter!

# Reuse your skills

Once you've mastered the basic projects in this book, think about how you could reuse those skills for new projects. Redecorate other items of furniture using the techniques used for the bedside cabinet on pages 16–17, or make a notebook in the same way as the diary on pages 8–9. You could also make a selection of cushions similar to the one on pages 14–15 using other clothes with fastenings, such as a zip-up top or a buttoned shirt.

The only limit to restyling your room is your imagination!

# Craft skills

## How to thread a needle

Cut a length of thread. Make sure it is no longer than your arm; too long a piece of thread will become knotted and make sewing hard work. Pass the tip of the thread through the eye of the needle. If the ends are frayed, dampen them slightly. Hold the two ends of thread together and loop into a knot. Doubling up the thread will help to make your sewing stronger.

## Starting and finishing a line of stitching

To start, fasten the thread to the fabric using a few backstitches.End a line of tacking with one backstitch or a knot.

## Sewing on buttons

Buttons usually have two or four holes, or have a single loop underneath. They need to be sewn on very firmly with plenty of stitches as they are generally subject to lots of wear and tear.

For a two-hole or looped button, sew through the holes or loop on to the fabric about six times in the same direction.
Tie off on the underside of the fabric.
For a four-hole button, use the same technique as for the two-hole button, using opposite holes to make a cross pattern.

## Tacking stitch

This is used to hold the fabric in position while it is being permanently stitched and is ideal for gathering fabric into ruffles. Pass the needle in and out of the fabric in a line to make long, even stitches.

**To make ruffles**, do not tie off the line of stitching, Gently pull the thread, sliding the fabric together into gathers or ruffles. When you have created the desired effect, tie off with a backstitch or knot.

## Running stitch

Similar to the tacking stitch, the running stitch uses smaller stitches. It is used for seams and for gathering and can also be used to decorative effect, particularly with wool or embroidery thread. You can stitch lines or curling patterns onto the surface of fabric.

Pass the needle in and out of the fabric in small, even stitches.

## Whipping stitch

This stitch is used to secure two pieces of fabric together at the edges.

Place two pieces of fabric on top of each other.

Fasten the thread to the inside of one piece of fabric. Pass the needle through both pieces of fabric from underneath, passing through where you have fastened the thread. Stitch through from the underside again to make a diagonal stitch about 1 cm from the first stitch.

## Blanket stitch

This is a decorative stitch used to bind the edge of fabric. Use a contrasting coloured thread for maximum effect.

Fasten the thread on the underside of the fabric, then pass the needle from the underside. Make a looped stitch over the edge of the fabric but before you pull it tight, pass the needle through the loop. Repeat.

# Glossary

**Accessory:** a fashion item such as jewellery, a scarf or a bag, that can be added to enhance your overall fashion look

**Biodegradable:** materials or substances that can be decomposed by natural bacteria

**Consumer:** a person who buys products and services for personal use

**Contaminant:** a toxic or poisonous substance that infects or dirties other substances

**Decompose:** the process by which man-made and natural materials and substances break down. It can be another word for rotting.

**Eco:** short for ecology; sometimes used in front of words to imply a positive effect on the environment, for example 'eco fashion'

**Environment:** the natural world, including air, soil, water, plants, and animals

**Landfill:** also known as a rubbish tip or dump, landfill is a site used for the disposal of waste materials

**Organic:** plants and animals that are grown or reared entirely naturally without the use of synthetic inputs such as pesticides, fertilizers and antibiotics

**Pesticide:** a chemical used to prevent, destroy or repel pests

**Pollution:** the release of environmental contaminants

**Recycle:** to use something again, usually after processing or remaking in some way

**Toxic:** poisonous

**Trend:** popular fashion or style at a given time

**Upcycle:** to take something that is disposable and transforming it into something of greater use and value

# Useful websites

**freecycle.org:** a website helping to keep unwanted consumer goods out of landfill. It brings together people who want to get rid of things and people who need those things.

**ebay.co.uk** an auction website where you can bid on other people's unwanted goods and possessions.

**etsy.com** a website where people can buy and sell handmade crafts. A great source for craft inspiration.

**folksy.com** a website where people can buy, sell and learn how to make handmade crafts.

**recyclethis.co.uk** an inspirational website with ideas on how to recycle, reuse and upcycle things that would otherwise go in the bin.

# Index

# eco chic

## Crafts for Accessorising That Look
978 0 7502 6834 9

Charm with your charms
Watch that bling!
Daisy button broach
Flutterby fascinator
Fabulous fluffy bangle
Sparkling velvet choker
Pretty pendant
Button bracelet
Mobile phone charm
Friendship anklet
Not any old hairband

## Crafts for Pampering Yourself
978 0 7502 6832 5

Wonderful wash bag/Fruity face mask
Bath-tastic flannel/Rose and coconut bath soak
Luscious lip balm and pot
Perfumed potpourri
Pampering pompom/body scrub
Homemade hair gel and pot
Lovely lavender bags
Funky fish soap dish/Make your own soap
Relaxing bath infusion
Bath bombs and gift box
Vanity kit

## Crafts for Revamping Your Room
978 0 7502 6844 8

Beanbag bookends
Dear diary
Personalised door sign
Pretty as a picture
Buttoned wool cushion
Bespoke bedroom cabinet
Bunting
Box of treasures
Sparkling CD hanger
Twinkling window mobile
Owl door stop

## Crafts for Styling Your Wardrobe
978 0 7502 6833 2

Tie-d together belt
Not just another plastic bag
Mac makeover
Scarf sensation
Gillet glamour
Perfect poncho
Groovy shoes
Transform a T-shirt
Make a skirt flirt!
Slipper chic
Dazzling jeans

WAYLAND